Editors

Kim Fields

Erica N. Russikoff, M.A.

Illustrator

Mark Mason

Cover Artist

Kevin Barnes

Barb Lorseyedi

Editor in Chief

Ina Massler Levin, M.A.

Creative Director

Karen J. Goldfluss, M.S. Ed.

Art Coordinator

Renée Christine Yates

Imaging

Rosa C. See

Publisher

Mary D. Smith, M.S. Ed.

Author

Garth Sundem, M.M.

Teacher Created Resources, Inc.

6421 Industry Way

Westminster, CA 92683

www.teachercreated.com

ISBN: 978-1-4206-2563-9

© *2009 Teacher Created Resources, Inc.*

Made in U.S.A.

Teacher Created Resources

Table of Contents

Table of Contents *(cont.)*

Introduction

Welcome to *Puzzles and Games That Make Kids Think*. This book contains over 185 puzzles and games of more than 30 different types, each of which is not only fun, but also asks students to use their minds to figure out the solution. (There are no "word finds" here!) Students will find some of these puzzles difficult, while other puzzles will be easy. Some puzzles will take seconds, while others might take half an hour. All of the puzzles are a workout for the brain! Here are a few reasons why we think you'll enjoy this book:

- Puzzle-based brain workouts create results. Research shows that a regimen of brainteasers can lead to higher scores on problem-solving tests.[1] Research also shows that using puzzles in the classroom can lead to increased student interest and involvement.[2]

- There are four categories of brainteasers in this book: picture, word, number, and logic, with puzzles (for individual students) and games (for pairs) for each category. Within each section, students will use diverse thinking skills—in a picture puzzle, students may draw lines on a geometric figure, and in a number puzzle, they may need to read complex directions. The wide variety of puzzles keeps students engaged and entertained.

- Each page of this book includes all of the needed directions and materials (other than writing utensils!), making it easy to distribute these puzzles to early finishers. Or, you may choose to copy and distribute puzzles as part of a reward system or weekly brain-buster challenge. Students will look forward to these fun puzzles, and you can rest assured that your classroom time will be spent productively. Another use of these puzzles is to spice up homework packets—strategically insert a puzzle or two to keep things lively!

- With a less experienced class, you may need to preview puzzle directions ahead of time (especially the two-person games and logic puzzles). Consider exploring the directions as a class before independent work time. Or, explain that reading and understanding the instructions is the first part of the puzzle! Because puzzle types repeat, students will gain more confidence in their ability to solve the puzzles as they spend more time with this book.

Be careful—these puzzles are addictive, and you can easily find yourself whiling away a prep period with pencil in hand!

[1] Howard, P. J. (1994). *The Owner's Manual for the Brain.* Charlotte, NC: Leornian Press.

[2] Finke, R. A., et al. (1992). *Creative Cognition: Theory, Research, and Applications.* Cambridge, MA: The MIT Press.

Puzzle Hints

Game Hints

Some games require the ability to read and understand somewhat difficult directions. Consider previewing directions with students beforehand. Also notice that some games require photocopying the page (or allowing students to cut shapes or game boards from the book). With less experienced classes, you might play a full-class version of a game (teacher versus students) before allowing pairs to work independently. In hopes of keeping game directions brief and student friendly, many of the more intuitive directions have been omitted. If students have questions about game mechanics, encourage them to use their common sense.

Picture Puzzles

- *Map Madness!:* Make sure you start at the correct point. Then, follow the route with your finger.
- *Rebus:* Where are words and/or pictures in relation to each other or to other elements? Say these relationships aloud and listen for common phrases.
- *Shape Find:* First, imagine the shape in your mind. Then, try to work around the figure systematically. And don't forget the whole figure itself!
- *Shape Slap:* Use the big shapes first. Place them in ways that will block your opponent.
- *Split Shapes:* Usually the lines are drawn from corners. Start there first.
- *Spun Shapes:* Imagine the first shape spun around the face of a clock. As it spins, which of the other shapes does it match? There is one shape that is different.
- *That's Not an Animal!:* Look for body parts borrowed from another animal (e.g., a hippo with antlers).
- *What's Different?:* Pretend there is a grid over each picture, and confine your search to only one box at a time.

Word Puzzles

- *Before and After:* If it doesn't come to you right away, brainstorm animals that would fit the correct number of boxes.
- *Changing Letters:* Pick the letter that you're going to try to change. If you can't think of something right away, scroll through the alphabet to see what fits. Think about *A*, then *B*, then *C*, then *D*, and go until something works.
- *Crack the Code:* Fill in each box in order. If you're running out of time, you can usually guess the answer before finishing the last few boxes.
- *Crossword:* Do the easy ones first. Then, use those letters to help you determine the more difficult ones.
- *Fronts and Backs:* Start with one "front" and then try it with each "back." Repeat this with each "front" on the list. Check off the "fronts" as you finish them.
- *Hide and Seek:* Scan the sentence slowly, looking for the names of different animals.
- *Letter Scramble:* Play with the vowel—it's usually the key.
- *Missing Letter:* Try the missing letter in every position, starting at the front and working your way through the word.
- *Transformers:* Look at the last word. Which letter from this word could be inserted in the first word to make a new word? Repeat until you get to the bottom.
- *Word Circles:* Most words start next to the vowel. Look there first.

Puzzle Hints *(cont.)*

Number Puzzles

- *Addition Challenge:* Start by adding big numbers and then finish with little numbers. This means you will work from the center to the outer boxes. In other words, add the nine, the eight, the seven, etc. until you get close to the number you need.

- *Fill in the Blanks:* Start on the right, with the singles digit, and then work left.

- *In Addition:* If there are three numbers in any row or column, you can find the fourth number. Do those first.

- *It's Touching:* First, look for rows or columns that are missing only one number. Then, look for shaded numbers with only one blank box touching.

- *Math Path:* You will almost always add the greatest numbers. In longer puzzles, look for a path between the two greatest numbers that includes an addition sign for both.

- *Operation Box:* Think of it in chunks, with two numbers and an equal sign. Fill in "chunks" with only one missing piece. Remember, there are no negatives!

- *Sudoku:* If a row, column, or 2 x 2 box already contains three numbers, you can fill in the fourth. Fill those in before proceeding.

- *Thinking of a Number:* Work from the filled-in digit.

Logic Puzzles

- *How Old?:* There are two things that have to be true. Try to figure out the first true thing, and then experiment with numbers that would also make the second thing true.

- *Jane's Watch, Anna's Kite, etc.:* Memorize the three things you are looking for (e.g., + stripes, + bows, – flowers). Then scan the puzzle in order, looking for the picture that matches the description.

- *Letter Box:* You will need to know the definitions of *row* and *column* to solve these.

- *Mike, Anita, and Jamal:* If two people did not do something, the third must have. If someone did something, it means that no one else did it and that he or she did not do anything else. (This will help you draw **X**s on the chart.)

- *Odd Animal Out:* Think about starting letters, or look for things that three of the animals have in common. Maybe there's more than one answer!

- *What's Next?:* Look for the repeating pattern.

Map Madness!

1

Do you see Jan? She is lost! Follow the directions to get her back on track.
Mark her ending spot with an **X**.

Directions:

1. ⬇️ Go south on Walnut Ave.   4. ⬅️ Go west on Hill St.

2. ➡️ Go east on Lake St.   5. **END** End at the corner of Almond Ave.

3. ⬆️ Go north on Peanut Ave.

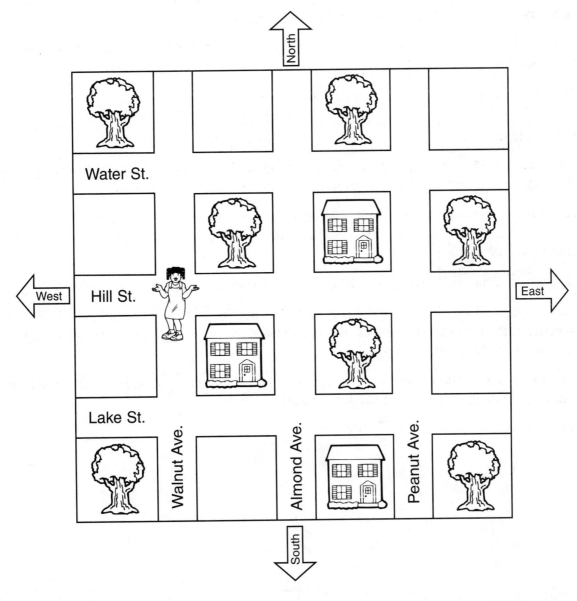

Spun Shapes

2

Which one of these shapes is not like the others? Circle it.

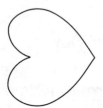   

Split Shapes

3

Can you draw five lines on this shape to make ten triangles?

Shape Find

4

How many circles can you find in this picture? _____

Crayon Game

5

Directions:

1. Put a red, blue, and green crayon in a bag, hat, or box.
2. Find a partner, and choose who goes first.
3. Pick a crayon from the bag. Don't peek!
4. Go to the next space on the board with that color. Color in that space. This space is now blocked. If the next space on the board is already colored (blocked), you can't land there, and you miss your turn. (If all of the "next" spaces in front of you are blocked, then you lose!)
5. Put the crayon back in the bag, hat, or box.
6. Take turns picking crayons until one of you reaches "FINISH." For the last move, stay at your spot until you pick the ending color.

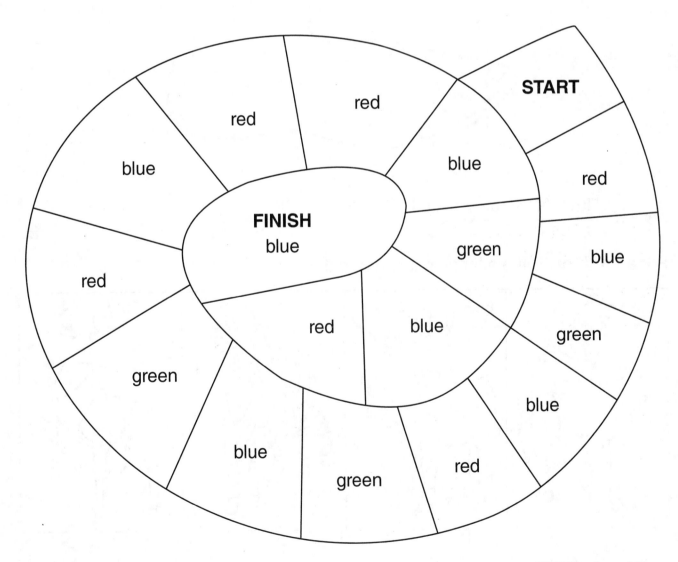

Split Shapes

6

Can you draw three lines on this shape to make four new triangles and two new rectangles?

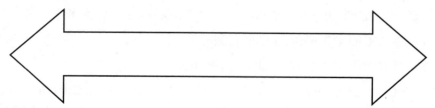

Rebus

7

This is a picture of a common saying. What is it? _____

That's Not an Animal!

8

Put an **X** through the animal that is not real.

Super Stumper: Split Shapes

9

Can you draw two lines on this shape to make five triangles?

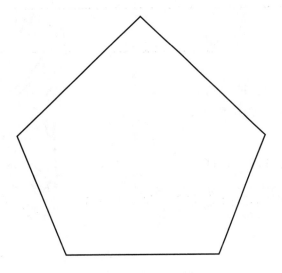

Columbus

10

This is a picture drawn when Columbus reached America. Can you find four things that don't belong? Circle them.

Brainstorm Game

11

Directions:

1. Find a partner. Then, look at the item on the right.

2. It is a net, but what else could it be?

3. You have 30 seconds to write one thing it could be on your set of lines. Be creative!

4. Now, it is your partner's turn.

5. Keep going until one person takes more than 30 seconds. The other person is the winner!

Player #1
_____
_____
_____
_____
_____
_____
_____
_____

Player #2
_____
_____
_____
_____
_____
_____
_____
_____

Split Shapes

12

Can you draw three lines on this shape to make seven triangles?

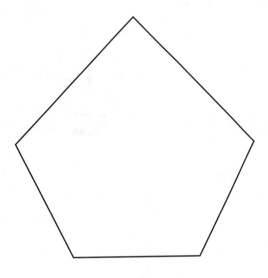

What's Different?

13

Can you spot the five differences between these two pictures? Circle them.

Map Madness!

Do you see Jan? She is lost again! Follow the directions to get her back on track. Mark her ending spot with an **X**.

Directions:

1. 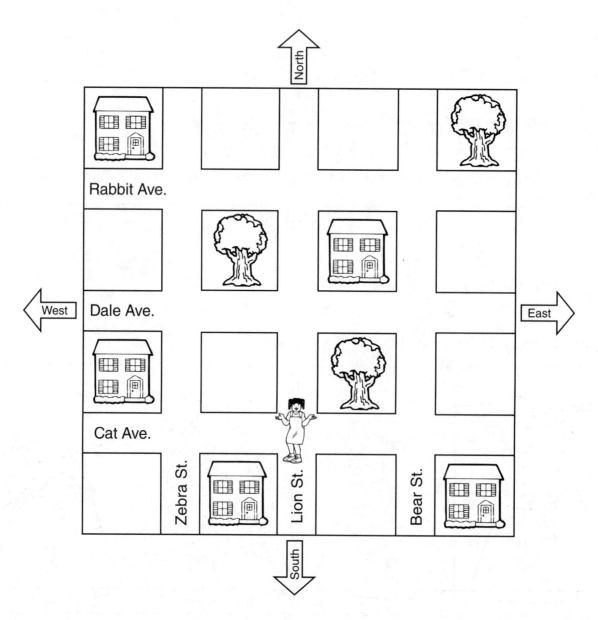 Go west on Cat Ave.

2. Go north on Zebra St.

3. Go east on Rabbit Ave.

4. Go south on Bear St.

5. **END** End at the corner of Cat Ave.

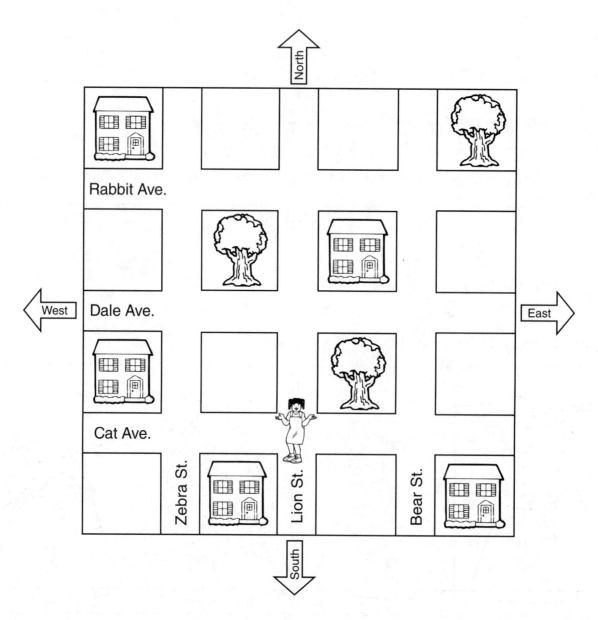

Split Shapes

15

Can you draw three lines on this shape to make nine triangles?

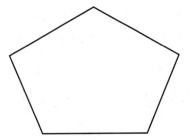

Rebus

16

This is a picture of a common saying. What is it? _____

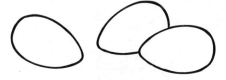

easy

That's Not an Animal!

17

Put an **X** through the animal that is not real.

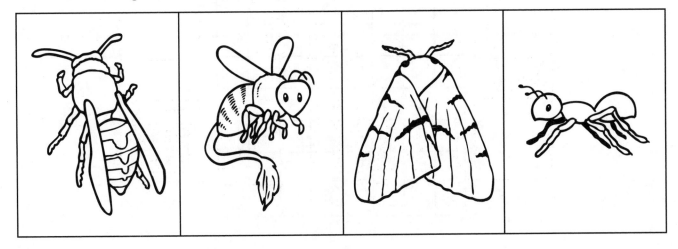

Shape Slap

18

Directions:

1. Find a partner. Look at the game board. Then, look at the shapes.

2. Pick a shape. Color in this shape on the board. If you need to, you can spin the shape. Draw an **X** over the shape you used.

3. Now, it is your partner's turn.

4. The first person who does not have room to place a shape loses!

Shapes:

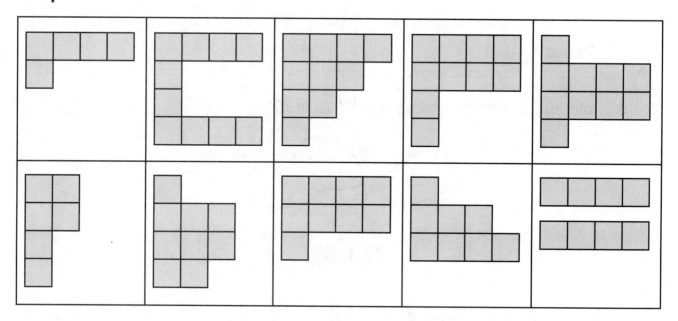

Game Board:

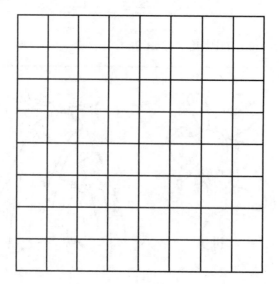

19 Split Shapes

Can you draw three lines on this shape to make nine triangles and one rectangle?

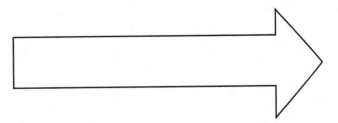

20 Shape Find

How many five-pointed stars can you find in this picture? _____

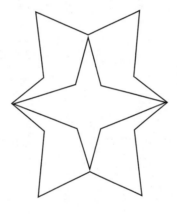

21 That's Not an Animal!

Put an **X** through the animal that is not real.

Spun Shapes

22

Which one of these shapes is not like the others? Circle it.

What's Different?

23

Can you spot the five differences between these two pictures? Circle them.

Rebus
24

This is a picture of a common saying. What is it? _____

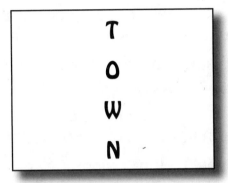

Super Stumper: Split Shapes
25

Can you draw three lines on this shape to make seven triangles?

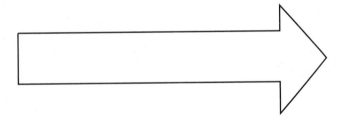

Super Stumper: Shape Find
26

How many squares can you find in this picture? _____

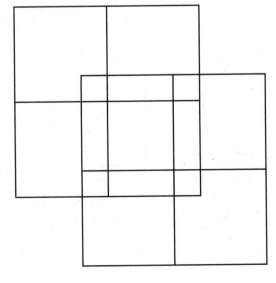

Tangram Game

Directions:

1. Find a partner. Each of you will need a copy of this sheet with your own set of shapes. Cut out the shapes in the square below.

2. Look at the tangram pictures below. When you say "go," you and your partner will race to make these pictures using all of your shapes.

3. Once one of you has made a picture, cross it out. This picture is now used. Both you and your partner should move on to the next picture.

4. Whoever makes the most pictures wins!

Shapes:

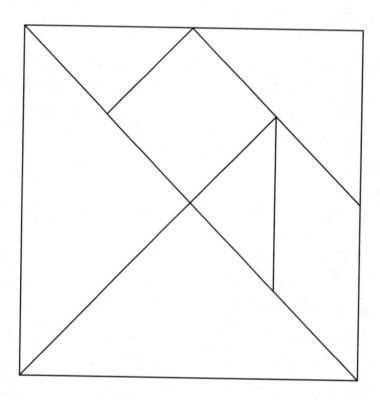

Tangram Pictures:

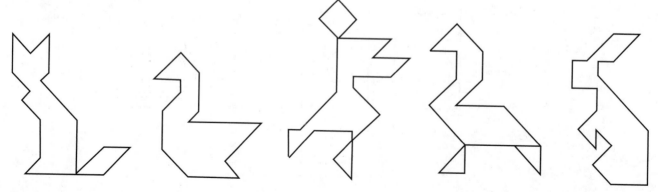

Map Madness!

Do you see Jan? She is lost! Follow the directions to get her back on track.
Mark her ending spot with an **X**.

Directions:

1. Go east on Easy St.

2. Go north on Green St.

3. Go west on Tricky St.

4. Go north on Red St.

5. **END** End at the corner of Hard St.

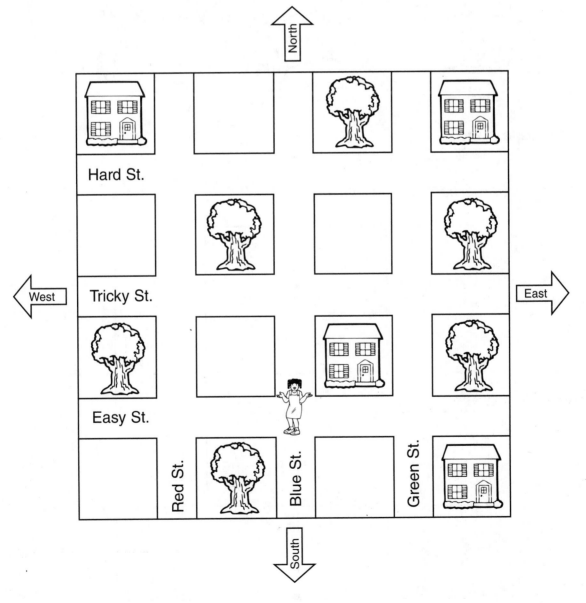

29 Pigs!

Can you find four things that don't belong in this picture? Circle them.

30 Shape Find

How many squares can you find in this picture? _____

Spun Shapes

31

Which one of these shapes is not like the others? Circle it.

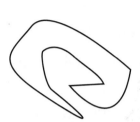   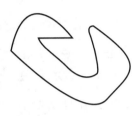

Shape Find

32

How many ovals can you find in this picture? _____

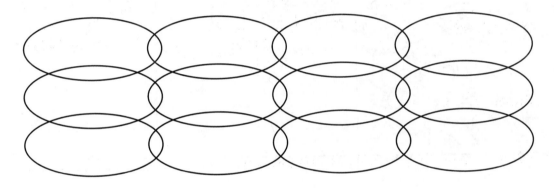

That's Not an Animal!

33

Put an **X** through the animal that is not real.

Cartoon Helpers

34

Directions:

1. Find a partner. You will each need a pencil.

2. Look at the boxes below. The first box shows the start of a cartoon.

3. Draw the next box. Then, have your partner write the caption for what you drew. Don't talk!

4. Now you will trade jobs: Your partner will draw the next box, and you will write the caption.

5. Take turns until all of the boxes are filled in.

6. At the end, work together to tell the complete story.

Pictures			
Captions	Molly and Chris went to the zoo.		

Pictures			
Captions			

35 What's Different?

Can you spot the five differences between these two pictures? Circle them.

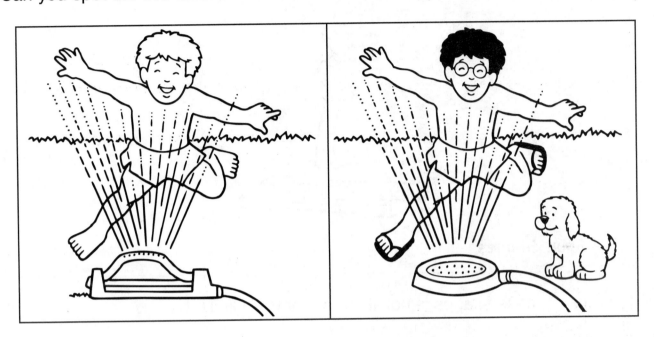

36 Split Shapes

Can you draw two lines on this shape to make eight triangles?

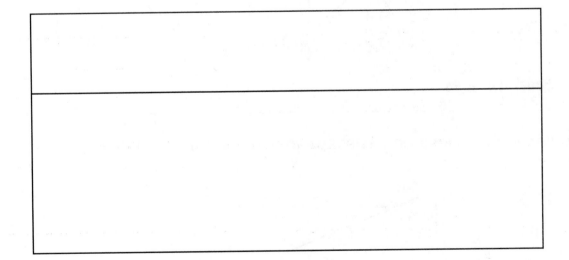

Rebus

37

This is a picture of a common saying. What is it? _____

Spun Shapes

38

Which one of these shapes is not like the others? Circle it.

Split Shapes

39

Can you draw three lines on this shape to make ten new triangles?

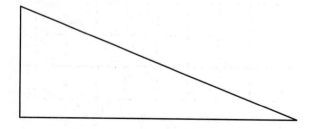

Shape Slap

40

Directions:

1. Find a partner. Look at the game board. Then, look at the shapes.
2. Pick a shape. Color in this shape on the board. If you need to, you can spin the shape. Draw an **X** over the shape you used.
3. Now, it is your partner's turn.
4. The first person who does not have room to place a shape loses!

Shapes:

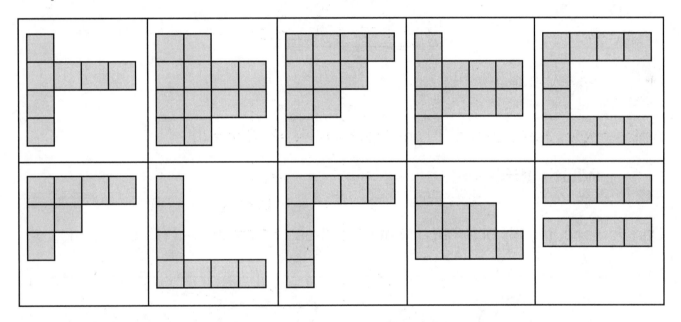

Game Board:

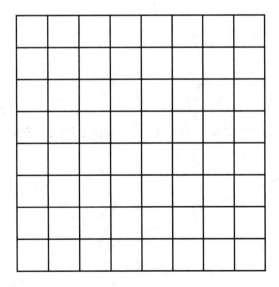

Split Shapes

Can you draw three lines on this shape to make three congruent triangles?

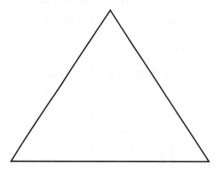

What's Different?

Can you spot the six differences between these two pictures? Circle them.

Shape Find
43

How many triangles can you find in this picture? _____

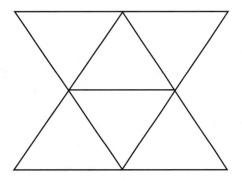

Spun Shapes
44

Which one of these shapes is not like the others? Circle it.

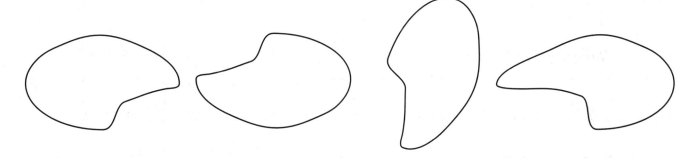

That's Not an Animal!
45

Put an **X** through the animal that is not real.

Map Madness!

Do you see Jan? She is lost! Follow the directions to get her back on track.
Mark her ending spot with an **X**.

Directions:

1. Go south on Caramel Ave.

2. Go east on Nut St.

3. Go north on Ice Cream Ave.

4. Go west on Peanut St.

5. Go north on Chocolate Ave.

6. **END** End at the corner of Almond St.

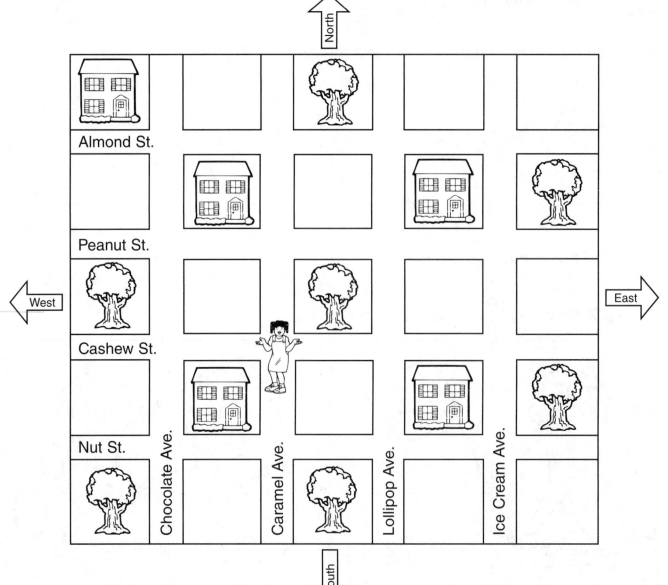

Triangle Take-Away Game

47

Directions:

1. Find a partner.

2. Put a blank piece of paper over the picture below, and trace it lightly in pencil.

3. Take turns erasing a line. You can erase a long or short line. But, you must leave at least one triangle.

4. The first person who cannot leave a triangle loses.

5. If you have time, trace the shape again and play another round!

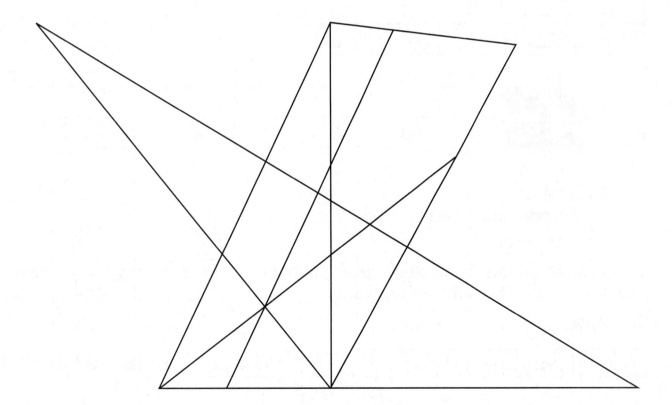

Letter Scramble

48

Make words using all of these letters: itps. Then, circle the words in the picture below.

1. _____

2. _____

3. _____

Crack the Code

49

What type of cat never plays fair? Crack the code to find out!

c	e	h	t	a
1	2	3	4	5

5	■	1	3	2	2	4	5	3

Before and After

50

Put an animal name in the blank boxes so that it makes a word or short phrase with the word in front and the word after.

Example:

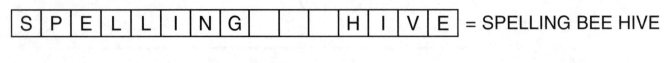

| S | P | E | L | L | I | N | G | | | H | I | V | E | = SPELLING BEE HIVE |

| L | U | C | K | Y | | | W | A | L | K |

Hide and Seek

51

Can you find the three animals hiding in this sentence? Circle them.

Example: Help igloos!

Charlotte requested a crown to cover her hairdo goof.

Missing Letter

52

The letter "t" has been taken out of the front, middle, or end of these words. The letter might be used more than once. What are the words?

pi:_____

sop: _____

ac: _____

oas: _____ , _____

es: _____

oher: _____

ogeher: _____

Crack the Code

53

What kind of test did the chicken take? Crack the code to find out!

z	n	e	m	a	g
1	2	3	4	5	6

5	2	■		3	6	6	1	5	4

Changing Letters
54

Directions:

1. Find a partner. Start with the word below.

2. Change one letter to make a new word. Write this word in the next row.

3. Take turns. You cannot use a word more than once.

4. If you cannot make a new word, you are out. When you reach the end of the puzzle together, you both win!

Example:

p	a	n
p	**i**	n
p	i	**g**
b	i	g

Start	b	i	g
1.			
2.			
3.			
4.			
5.			
6.			
7.			
8.			
9.			
10.			

55 Missing Letter

The letter "n" has been taken out of the front, middle, or end of these words. The letter might be used more than once. What are the words?

ope: _____, _____   ie: _____

o: _____, _____   eed: _____

stu: _____   ose: _____

56 Letter Scramble

Make words using all of these letters: isft. Then, circle one of the words in the picture below.

1. _____

2. _____

3. _____

Flour

57 Crossword

Read the clues and fill in the letters.

Across

  1. to get, in the past
  4. a historical period
  5. more than one man

Down

  1. a valuable stone
  2. rocks containing metal
  3. what you get when lying in the sun

1	2	3
4		
5		

58 Hide and Seek

Can you find the three animals hiding in this sentence? Circle them.

Example: Help igloos!

Catherine ran to and fro, going home.

59 Before and After

Put an animal name in the blank boxes so that it makes a word or short phrase with the word in front and the word after.

Example:

| S | P | E | L | L | I | N | G | | | H | I | V | E | = SPELLING BEE HIVE |

| E | A | R | L | Y | | | | B | R | A | I | N |

60 Transformers

Change one letter at a time to get from the top word to the bottom word. Each row must make a real word.

Example:

p	a	n
p	i	n
p	i	**g**
b	i	g

h	e	n
p	o	t

Fronts and Backs

61

Directions:

1. These letters are the "fronts" and "backs" of words.
2. Find a partner. Make a word using the "fronts" and "backs" provided. Write it in your space.
3. Take turns writing words.
4. If you cannot make a new word, you are out.
5. The person with the most words wins!

Fronts	Backs
co	mb
to	ach
gro	ast
bo	uch
fe	st
be	ss
	gin
	lt

Player #1	Player #2

Hide and Seek
62

Can you find the three animals hiding in this sentence? Circle them.

Example: Hel(p ig)loos!

Tou can't eat erasers or giant cookies.

Missing Letter
63

The letter "w" has been taken out of the front, middle, or end of these words. What are the words?

on: _____, _____   mo:_____

ill: _____   ol:_____

ing: _____   bol:_____

Crossword
64

Read the clues and fill in the letters.

Across

1. the opposite of *on*
4. what you breathe
5. to attempt

Down

1. a grain
2. a tree with green needles
3. to cook in oil

1	2	3
4		
5		

Letter Scramble

65

Make words using all of these letters: scta. Then, circle the words in the picture below.

1. _____

2. _____

3. _____

4. _____

Word Circles

66

Start at any letter. Go left or right. What games can you spell? Write them in the circles.

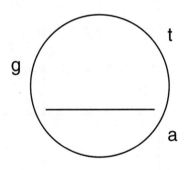

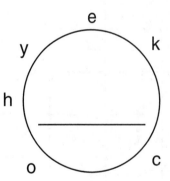

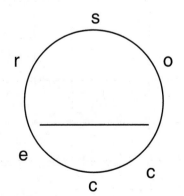

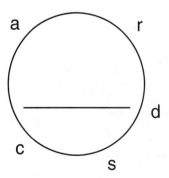

Crossword Challenge

67

Directions:

1. Using different-colored pens, work with a partner to put these words into the crossword puzzle. Each word must touch at least one other word.

2. Now, take turns adding new words to the puzzle. Be creative!

3. The person who can add the most new words wins.

Ohio   TENNESSEE

Maine   **Alaska**   Washington

A	L	A	B	A	M	A			

Crack the Code

68

What type of cat never tells the truth? Crack the code to find out!

i	a	l	o	n
1	2	3	4	5

2	■	3	1	4	5

Hide and Seek

69

Can you find the three animals hiding in this sentence? Circle them.

Example: Help igloos!

Fido got terrible fleas.

Super Stumper: Transformers

70

Change one letter at a time to get from the top word to the bottom word.
Each row must make a real word.

Example:

p	a	n
p	**i**	n
p	i	**g**
b	i	g

o	n	e
o	i	l

Before and After

71

Put an animal name in the blank boxes so that it makes a word or short phrase with the word in front and the word after.

Example:

S	P	E	L	L	I	N	G			H	I	V	E

= SPELLING BEE HIVE

	L	I	T	T	L	E					B	A	N	K

Missing Letter

72

The letter "r" has been taken out of the front, middle, or end of these words. The letter might be used more than once. What are the words?

ip: _____

wappe: _____

sting: _____

bing: _____

stinge: _____ , _____

stange: _____ , _____

ange: _____ , _____ ,

_____

Crossword

73

Read the clues and fill in the letters.

Across

  1. It hangs from a basketball hoop.

  4. a paddle

  5. the opposite of *wet*

Down

  1. to bob your head

  2. what you hear with

  3. to attempt

1	2	3
4		
5		

Word Circles

Start at a letter. Go left or right. What states can you spell? Write them in the circles.

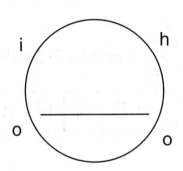

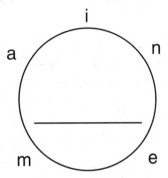

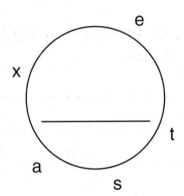

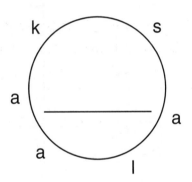

Crack the Code

I have a tail and a head, but no body. I am not a snake. What am I?

Crack the code to find out!

u	a	q	e	r	t
1	2	3	4	5	6

2	■	3	1	2	5	6	4	5

Beginnings and Ends Game

Directions:

1. Find a partner.

2. Look at the pictures below. Think of the words they show.

3. Start at *mouse*. This word ends with the letter "e." Which word begins with the letter "e"? The first one has been done for you.

4. Take turns drawing arrows to the next picture. Also, write the words you use.

5. If you cannot find a word in one minute, your partner wins. If you can use every picture, you both win!

Crossword

77

Read the clues and fill in the letters.

Across

  1. a grain

  4. It happened long _____.

  5. You use it to open a lock.

Down

  1. a large tree

  2. how old you are

  3. You play with it.

1	2	3
4		
5		

Hide and Seek

78

Can you find the three animals hiding in this sentence? Circle them.

Example: Help igloos!

The crowded room was packed with ogres!

Transformers

79

Change one letter at a time to get from the top word to the bottom word. Each row must make a real word.

Example:

p	a	n
p	i	n
p	i	**g**
b	i	g

c	o	w
b	i	g

80 Missing Letter

The letter "r" has been taken out of the front, middle, or end of these words. The letter might be used more than once. What are the words?

at: _____ , _____   aft: _____

ca: _____   afte: _____

stat: _____   ound: _____

81 Letter Scramble

Make words using all of these letters: sten. Then, circle the words in the picture below.

1. _____

2. _____

3. _____

4. _____

82 Before and After

Put an animal name in the blank boxes so that it makes a word or short phrase with the word in front and the word after.

Example:

S	P	E	L	L	I	N	G			H	I	V	E

= SPELLING BEE HIVE

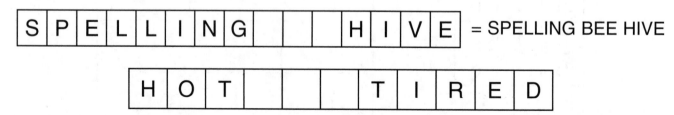

Hide and Seek

83

Can you find the three animals hiding in this sentence? Circle them.

Example: Hel(p ig)loos!

The commando granny told the doc to push with a crowbar.

Word Circles

84

Start at any letter. Go left or right. What fruits can you spell? Write them in the circles.

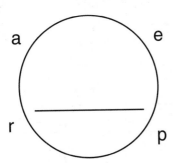

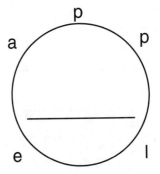

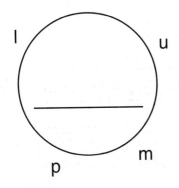

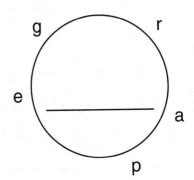

Fronts and Backs

85

Directions:

1. These letters are the "fronts" and "backs" of words.

2. Find a partner. Make a word using the "fronts" and "backs" provided. Write it in your space.

3. Take turns writing words.

4. If you cannot make a new word, you are out.

5. The person with the most words wins!

Fronts	Backs
thr	ough
en	ead
alth	oat
spr	ifty
b	emy
n	ain
	ing

Player #1	Player #2

Hide and Seek
86

Can you find the two animals hiding in this sentence? Circle them.

Example: Help igloos!

Do girls have pigtails?

Transformers
87

Change one letter at a time to get from the top word to the bottom word. Each row must make a real word.

Example:

p	a	n
p	i	n
p	i	**g**
b	i	g

p	e	n
l	o	g

Crossword
88

Read the clues and fill in the letters.

Across

1. a light brown
4. It happened long _____.
5. to obtain

Down

1. a popular playground game
2. how old you are
3. The wrong answer is _____ right.

1	2	3
4		
5		

89 **Letter Scramble**

Make words using all of these letters: pste. Then, circle the words in the picture below.

1. _____

2. _____

3. _____

Now, use the words to write a sentence that describes the picture.

_____

_____

90 **Crossword**

Read the clues and fill in the letters.

Across

1. _____ End

4. a long, skinny fish

5. what a dog says

Down

1. a hot drink

2. Annie cut _____ hair.

3. a small fairy-tale creature

1	2	3
4		
5		

Crack the Code

91

Which side of a cat has the most hair? Crack the code to find out!

u	t	s	e	h	i	o	d
1	2	3	4	5	6	7	8

			■						
2	5	4		7	1	2	3	6	8	4

Word Circles

92

Start at any letter. Go left or right. What meals can you spell? Write them in the circles.

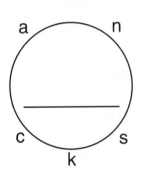 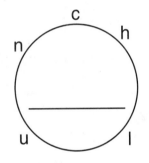 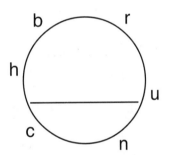 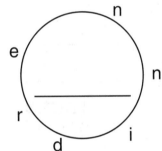

Crossword

93

Read the clues and fill in the letters.

Across

1. A spider weaves its _____.

4. a climbing plant

5. Golly _____!

Down

1. fake hair

2. the day before

3. the opposite of "hi!"

1	2	3
4		
5		

Rhyme Game

94

Directions:

1. Find a partner. Each player should use a different-colored pen. Then, look at the words below.

2. Race your partner to write rhymes for these words. Remember, words don't have to be spelled the same in order to rhyme!

3. Once you write a rhyme in a box, the box is closed.

4. Whoever closes the most boxes wins!

5. If you have time, work together to write a poem using some of these words.

feather	mother	spring
rhyme	rhyme	rhyme
freeze	muscle	handle
rhyme	rhyme	rhyme
book	trouble	route
rhyme	rhyme	rhyme
mouse	stinger	band
rhyme	rhyme	rhyme

Crack the Code
95

What happens when a duck flies upside down? Crack the code to find out!

a	s	c	i	u	t	k	q	p
1	2	3	4	5	6	7	8	9

		■						■		
4	6		8	5	1	3	7	2	5	9

Word Circles
96

Start at any letter. Go left or right. What animals can you spell? Write them in the circles.

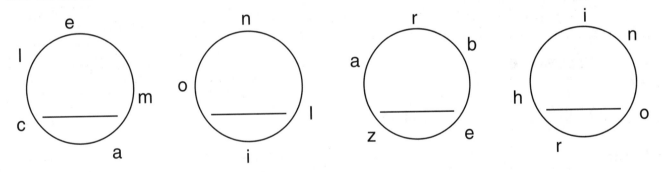

Before and After
97

Put an animal name in the blank boxes so that it makes a word or short phrase with the word in front and the word after.

Example:

| S | P | E | L | L | I | N | G | | | H | I | V | E | = SPELLING BEE HIVE |

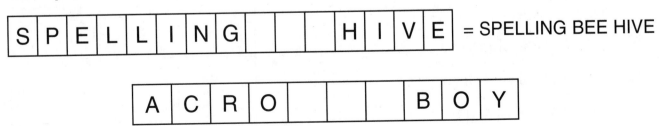

Letter Scramble

98

Make two words using all of these letters: tca. Then, circle one of the words in the picture below.

1. _____

2. _____

Now, use the words to write a sentence that describes the picture.

_____

_____

_____

Crossword

99

Read the clues and fill in the letters.

Across

1. It holds up your pants.

5. the opposite of *under*

6. _____ and shine!

7. Or _____!

Down

1. to drill a hole

2. the opposite of *good*

3. the opposite of *more*

4. It has leaves and bark.

1	2	3	4
5			
6			
7			

Transformers

100

Change one letter at a time to get from the top word to the bottom word.
Each row must make a real word.

Example:

p	e	s	t
p	**o**	s	t
p	o	**e**	t
p	o	e	**m**

r	i	s	e
h	o	m	e

Word Circles

101

Start at a letter. Go left or right. What countries can you spell? Write them in the circles.

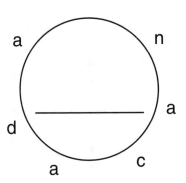

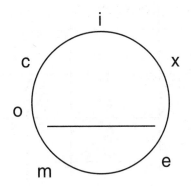

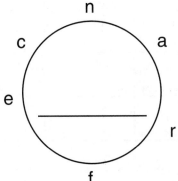

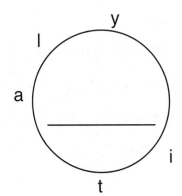

Changing Letters

102

Directions:

1. Find a partner.

2. Start with the word below. Then, change one letter to make a new word. Write the word in the next row.

3. Take turns. You cannot use a word more than once.

4. If you cannot make a new word, you are out. When you reach the end of the puzzle, you both win!

Example:

p	a	n
p	**i**	n
p	i	**g**
b	i	g

Start	**r**	**i**	**n**	**g**
1.				
2.				
3.				
4.				
5.				
6.				
7.				
8.				
9.				
10.				

103 Sudoku

Each row, column, and 2 x 2 box has the numbers 1, 2, 3, and 4. Fill in the blanks to complete the puzzle.

	4	3	2
3		1	4
2	1		3
4	3	2	

104 In Addition

Fill in the blanks with the numbers 1–9 so that the sum of each row is the number to the right, and the sum of each column is the number below it.

		5		20
9	6		6	24
7	4	2	7	20
	9		3	22

25	26	14	21

105 Fill in the Blanks

Fill in the blanks to make this equation true.

$$
\begin{array}{cccc}
  & 1 & 6 & 9 \\
+ &   & \Box & 7 \\
\hline
  & \Box & 3 & \Box \\
\end{array}
$$

106 Thinking of a Number

I'm thinking of a four-digit number in which:

- each digit is two less than the digit before it.

		3	

107 Operation Box

Fill in each blank box with a number so that everything that touches is true and positive.

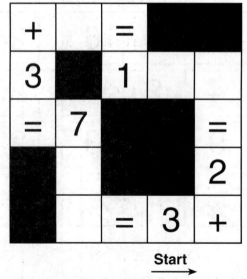

Start →

Addition Challenge

108

Directions:

1. Pick a colored pen. Have your partner pick a different color.
2. One player is on the left, and one player is on the right.
3. Look at the numbers in the middle. In each row, circle the numbers on your side that add up to the number in the middle. You can circle as many numbers as you need. For example:

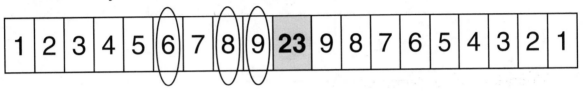

4. Once you have circled any combination of numbers, put an **X** on the number in the middle. That row is now closed. You get a point for each **X**.
5. Start at the same time, and solve as many rows as you can before your partner.
6. You do not have to solve the rows in order. (You can start at the end or skip around.)
7. At the end, the person with the most points wins.

Player #1										Player #2								
1	2	3	4	5	6	7	8	9	**12**	9	8	7	6	5	4	3	2	1
1	2	3	4	5	6	7	8	9	**21**	9	8	7	6	5	4	3	2	1
1	2	3	4	5	6	7	8	9	**19**	9	8	7	6	5	4	3	2	1
1	2	3	4	5	6	7	8	9	**27**	9	8	7	6	5	4	3	2	1
1	2	3	4	5	6	7	8	9	**34**	9	8	7	6	5	4	3	2	1
1	2	3	4	5	6	7	8	9	**16**	9	8	7	6	5	4	3	2	1
1	2	3	4	5	6	7	8	9	**26**	9	8	7	6	5	4	3	2	1

109 Math Path

Pick the best starting number, and then go up/down or left/right until you have touched all of the spaces once. What is the *highest* total you can end with? Draw your path.

2	–	1
+	2	
2	+	

Total: _____

110 It's Touching

Fill in the blank boxes with the numbers 1–5. Each full row and column contains the numbers 1, 2, 3, 4, and 5. Each shaded number is the sum of all the numbers touching it.

5		3	1	
4	33	5	21	3
3	5		2	
1	21	2	24	5
2		1		4

Fill in the Blanks

111

Fill in the blanks to make this equation true.

$$
\begin{array}{r}
1\ \ 6\ \ \boxed{} \\
+\quad\ \ 8\ \ 7 \\
\hline
\boxed{}\ \boxed{}\ 5
\end{array}
$$

Operation Box

112

Fill in each blank box with a number so that everything that touches is true and positive.

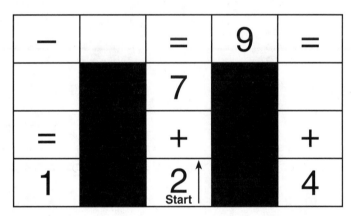

Thinking of a Number

113

I'm thinking of a four-digit number in which:

- the third digit is three more than the first.

- the second digit is one less than the third.

- the fourth digit is three more than the third.

114 Sudoku

Each row, column, and 2 x 2 box has the numbers 1, 2, 3, and 4. Fill in the blanks to complete the puzzle.

2		1	
1	3		4
3		4	
	1	3	2

115 Math Path

Pick the best starting number, and then go up/down or left/right until you have touched all of the spaces once. What is the *highest* total you can end with? Draw your path.

2	–	1
–	2	
1	+	

Total: _____

Tic-Tac-Toe Race

Directions:

1. Pick a colored pen. Have your partner pick a different color.

2. Choose a tic-tac-toe board, and sit side by side.

3. Start at the same time, and race to solve the math problems.

4. When you solve a problem, write the answer in the box.

5. If you get three in a row, you win!

6. Check your answers. If your partner wrote a wrong answer, the space is yours!

Example:

6 – 4	4 + 2	8 – 3
9 + 5 14	4 + 5	2 + 7
1 + 6	3 + 9	7 – 5

Game Boards:

5 + 13	2 x 7	8 – 5
72 – 34	34 + 17	4 x 9
56 + 32	84 – 43	2 x 3

31 + 47	4 x 6	22 – 16
3 – 2	33 – 22	7 x 8
7 x 4	18 + 26	31 – 14

53 – 35	32 + 23	3 x 9
6 x 4	16 + 26	91 – 19
1 x 21	82 – 28	22 + 34

42 + 49	33 – 16	4 x 8
28 – 17	8 x 5	52 + 23
5 x 7	14 + 18	66 – 33

In Addition

117

Fill in the blanks with the numbers 1–9 so that the sum of each row is the number to the right, and the sum of each column is the number below it.

			11
4	2		**11**
8		4	**19**
15	**14**	**12**	

It's Touching

118

Fill in the blank boxes with the numbers 1–5. Each full row and column contains the numbers 1, 2, 3, 4, and 5. Each shaded number is the sum of all the numbers touching it.

	2		1	
1	23	2	23	3
2	5		4	
4	27	4	24	5
	3	1	4	

119 Thinking of a Number

I'm thinking of a four-digit number in which:

- the sum of the first two digits is eight.
- the sum of all the digits is seventeen.

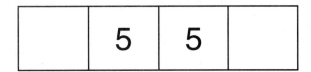

120 Fill in the Blanks

Fill in the blanks to make this equation true.

$$
\begin{array}{r}
\boxed{}\ \boxed{}\ 7 \\
+\qquad 9\ \ 9 \\
\hline
4\ \ 5\ \ \boxed{} \\
\end{array}
$$

121 Operation Box

Fill in each blank box with a number so that everything that touches is true and positive.

Start

7	−	2	=
=	■	■	5
	■	■	+
−	16	=	

122 Sudoku

Each row, column, and 2 x 2 box has the numbers 1, 2, 3, and 4. Fill in the blanks to complete the puzzle.

1	3	2	
		1	3
	1		2
	2	4	1

123 In Addition

Fill in the blanks with the numbers 1–9 so that the sum of each row is the number to the right, and the sum of each column is the number below it.

	6	4	12
5			18
		1	9

10	17	12

Snake Race

124

Directions:

1. Find a partner. Each player should use a different-colored pen.

2. Sit side by side, and put the game board in front of you.

3. Look for snakes that add up to thirteen. The numbers have to be touching. (You cannot jump around.) Once a number is taken, you cannot use it again.

4. Take turns. You have 30 seconds to find a snake.

5. If you cannot find a snake in 30 seconds, the other person wins.

Example:

5	+	4	+
+	3	+	4
7	+	6	+
+	3	+	8

Game Board:

4	+	2	+	4	+	3
+	1	+	5	+	4	+
3	+	2	+	5	+	6
+	7	+	2	+	1	+
2	+	1	+	4	+	3
+	2	+	5	+	6	+
3	+	2	+	5	+	3

Fill in the Blanks
125

Fill in the blanks to make this equation true.

$$
\begin{array}{r}
\boxed{}\ \boxed{}\ 9 \\
+\qquad 4\ \ 3 \\
\hline
4\quad 2\ \ \boxed{}
\end{array}
$$

Thinking of a Number
126

I'm thinking of a four-digit number in which:

- the sum of the first and last digit is fourteen.
- the sum of the first and second digit is fifteen.
- the sum of all the digits is twenty-five.

			5

Operation Box
127

Fill in each blank box with a number so that everything that touches is true and positive.

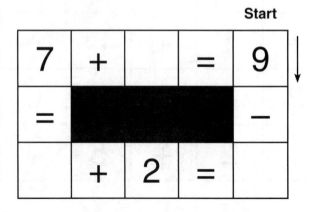

Sudoku
128

Each row, column, and 2 x 2 box has the numbers 1, 2, 3, and 4. Fill in the blanks to complete the puzzle.

1	2	4	
	3		2
3			
	4	3	1

In Addition
129

Fill in the blanks with the numbers 1–9 so that the sum of each row is the number to the right, and the sum of each column is the number below it.

1			15
	3		13
2		5	13

9	18	14

130 ## Thinking of a Number

I'm thinking of a four-digit number in which:

- the first digit is three less than the third.
- the third digit is two more than the second.
- the fourth digit is twice the first.

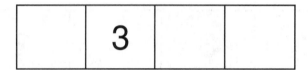

131 ## Fill in the Blanks

Fill in the blanks to make this equation true.

$$\begin{array}{ccc} \square & 7 & \square \\ + & 6 & 5 \\ \hline 7 & \square & 2 \end{array}$$

132 ## Operation Box

Fill in each blank box with a number so that everything that touches is true and positive.

+	2	=	
		6↑ Start	3
=			=
	−		
	1	=	5	−

Addition Challenge

Directions:

1. Pick a colored pen. Have your partner pick a different color.

2. One player is on the left, and one player is on the right.

3. Look at the numbers in the middle. In each row, circle the numbers on your side that add up to the number in the middle. You can circle as many numbers as you need. For example:

1	2	3	4	5	6	7	8	9	**23**	9	8	7	6	5	4	3	2	1

4. Once you have circled any combination of numbers, put an **X** on the number in the middle. That row is now closed. You get a point for each **X**.

5. Start at the same time, and solve as many rows as you can before your partner.

6. You do not have to solve the rows in order. (You can start at the end or skip around.)

7. At the end, the person with the most points wins.

Player #1										Player #2								
2	3	4	5	6	7	8	9	10	**22**	10	9	8	7	6	5	4	3	2
2	3	4	5	6	7	8	9	10	**35**	10	9	8	7	6	5	4	3	2
2	3	4	5	6	7	8	9	10	**47**	10	9	8	7	6	5	4	3	2
2	3	4	5	6	7	8	9	10	**19**	10	9	8	7	6	5	4	3	2
2	3	4	5	6	7	8	9	10	**39**	10	9	8	7	6	5	4	3	2
2	3	4	5	6	7	8	9	10	**49**	10	9	8	7	6	5	4	3	2
2	3	4	5	6	7	8	9	10	**32**	10	9	8	7	6	5	4	3	2

Math Path

134

Pick the best starting number and then go up/down or left/right until you have touched all of the spaces once. What is the *highest* total you can end with? Draw your path.

–	3	–	1
1	+	4	

Total: _____

Sudoku

135

Each row, column, and 2 x 2 box has the digits 1, 2, 3, and 4. Fill in the blanks to complete the puzzle.

	2		4
1	4	3	2
4	3	2	1
2		4	

136 **It's Touching**

Fill in the blank boxes with the numbers 1–5. Each full row and column contains the numbers 1, 2, 3, 4, and 5. Each shaded number is the sum of all the numbers touching it.

	3	1	4	5
5	21		27	2
	2	4	5	3
3	26		27	
4		2	3	1

137 **In Addition**

Fill in the blanks with the numbers 1–9 so that the sum of each row is the number to the right, and the sum of each column is the number below it.

		4	9
2	6		16
	7		17

11	16	15

Plus or Minus Game

138

Directions:

1. Find a partner. Each of you will need a copy of this sheet 101 and a different-colored pen.
2. Look at the rows below. In each row, you have to add and/or subtract to get from the first number to the last. The first one has been done for you.
3. Race your partner to solve the rows. You do not have to go in order. The person who solves the most rows wins.
4. Ready, set, go!

8	+ or ⊖	3	⊕ or −	2	=	7
28	+ or −	7	+ or −	9	=	30
32	+ or −	12	+ or −	5	=	15
19	+ or −	6	+ or −	1	=	24
40	+ or −	30	+ or −	10	=	20
16	+ or −	1	+ or −	8	=	7
25	+ or −	13	+ or −	3	=	35
11	+ or −	4	+ or −	2	=	17

Sudoku

139

Each row, column, and 2 x 2 box has the digits 1, 2, 3, and 4. Fill in the blanks to complete the puzzle.

2		1	
1	4	2	3
4	2	3	1
	1		2

Math Path

140

Pick the best starting number, and then go up/down or left/right until you have touched all of the spaces once. What is the *highest* total you can end with? Draw your path.

3	–	4
–	1	+
4	–	2

Total: _____

141 In Addition

Fill in the blanks with the numbers 1–9 so that the sum of each row is the number to the right, and the sum of each column is the number below it.

5				16
		4		12
4	2			12

15	13	12

142 It's Touching

Fill in the blank boxes with the numbers 1–5. Each full row and column contains the numbers 1, 2, 3, 4, and 5. Each shaded number is the sum of all the numbers touching it.

	3	2		4
5	21	1	24	
	4	3	1	5
4	26	5	26	
	1	4	5	2

143 Thinking of a Number

I'm thinking of a four-digit number in which:

- the last digit is three times the first.
- the second digit is the sum of the first and last.
- the third digit is two more than the first.

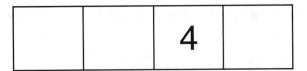

144 Fill in the Blanks

Fill in the blanks to make this equation true.

$$\begin{array}{r} \boxed{}\ \boxed{}\ 7 \\ +\ \ \ \ 7\ \ 4 \\ \hline 6\ \ 3\ \ \boxed{} \end{array}$$

145 Operation Box

Fill in each blank box with a number so that everything that touches is true and positive.

8	=		+	6
−	■	■	■	=
1	■	7↓ Start	■	
=	■	+	■	−
	■		=	9

Meet Your Match

146

Directions:

1. Find a partner. Each of you will need a copy of this sheet and a different-colored pen.
2. Look at the left and right sides in the columns below. On each side, there are equations that have the same answer.
3. Draw lines between equations that have the same answer. The first one has been done for you.
4. The person who can draw the most lines wins.

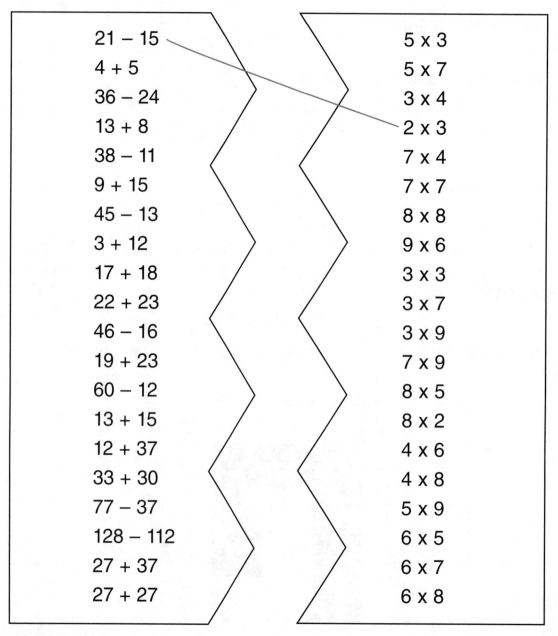

21 – 15	5 x 3
4 + 5	5 x 7
36 – 24	3 x 4
13 + 8	2 x 3
38 – 11	7 x 4
9 + 15	7 x 7
45 – 13	8 x 8
3 + 12	9 x 6
17 + 18	3 x 3
22 + 23	3 x 7
46 – 16	3 x 9
19 + 23	7 x 9
60 – 12	8 x 5
13 + 15	8 x 2
12 + 37	4 x 6
33 + 30	4 x 8
77 – 37	5 x 9
128 – 112	6 x 5
27 + 37	6 x 7
27 + 27	6 x 8

78

In Addition

147

Fill in the blanks with the numbers 1–9 so that the sum of each row is the number to the right, and the sum of each column is the number below it.

		8	12
4	2		15
8			19

15	7	24

Math Path

148

Pick the best starting number and then go up/down or left/right until you have touched all of the spaces once. What is the *highest* total you can end with? Draw your path.

2	+	6
−	4	+
5	+	7

Total: _____

Sudoku

149

Each row, column, and 2 x 2 box has the digits 1, 2, 3, and 4. Fill in the blanks to complete the puzzle.

	3	4	
4		2	
1			
	4	1	2

In Addition

150

Fill in the blanks with the numbers 1–9 so that the sum of each row is the number to the right, and the sum of each column is the number below it.

4		7	2	16
6	5	2		14
2		3	5	19
	4			20

20	21	14	14

How Old?

151

Karen's brother is three years older than she is.

He is twelve years old.

How old will Karen be in four years? _____

Letter Box

152

Put the letters A, C, and D in the boxes so that:

- A and D are in the same column.
- A and B are in the same row.

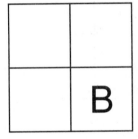

Odd Animal Out

153

Circle the animal that does not belong.

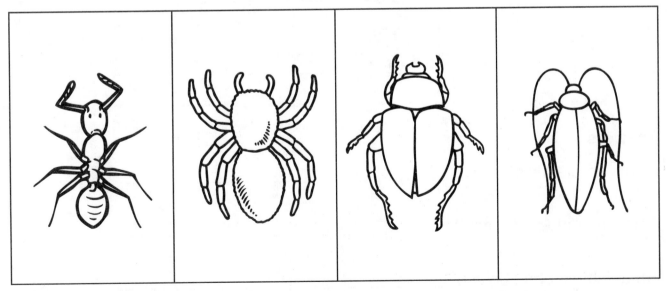

Why doesn't it belong? _____

Mike, Anita, and Jamal

154

Mike, Anita, and Jamal caught fish. Read each clue. Then, mark the chart to see who caught which fish.

Clues:

✔ Anita caught the large fish.

✔ Mike did not catch the small fish.

Example:

	Walk	Run	Jump
Mary		✕	✕
Seth	✕	✕	
Rich	✕		✕

Chart:

	Small Fish	Medium Fish	Large Fish
Mike			
Anita			
Jamal			

Answers:

What fish did Mike catch? _____

What fish did Anita catch? _____

What fish did Jamal catch? _____

82

Four-in-a-Row

155

Directions:

1. Find a partner.
2. Choose **X**s or **O**s.
3. Take turns putting an **X** or an **O** in a box.
4. Try to make four in a row, either up-and-down or right-and-left (no diagonals).
5. At the end, count how many four-in-a-rows you made. The person who makes the most wins.
6. If you have time, play again!

Example:

X	X	X	X	O	O
O	O	X	X	O	O
X	X	X	X	O	O
X	X	X	X	O	X
O	O	O	O	X	O
O	O	X	O	O	X

Game Boards:

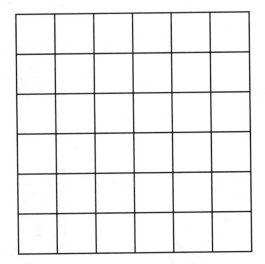

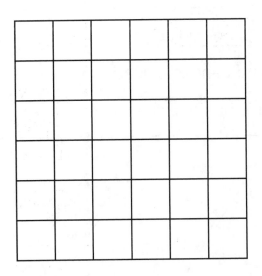

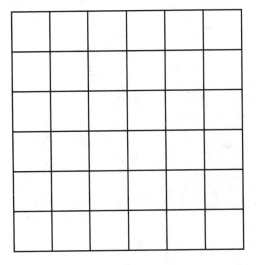

Letter Box

156

Put the letters A, B, and C in the boxes so that:

- A is in the bottom row.
- C is in the left column.

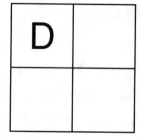

Jane's Watch

157

Jane lost her watch. Can you help her find it? Circle the correct watch.

Here are facts about Jane's watch:

 It is not digital.

 The band is striped.

 It is has a circular face.

What's Next?

158

Draw the shape that should come next.

How Old?

159

Jim's little sister is four. In two years,

Jim will be twice as old as she is now.

How old is Jim now? _____

Odd Animal Out

160

Circle the animal that does not belong.

Why doesn't it belong? _____

Add One or Two

Directions:

1. Find a partner. Each player should use a different-colored pen.

2. Look at the boxes below.

3. Take turns coloring in boxes.

4. You can color in either one or two boxes per turn.

5. Whoever colors in the last box wins.

Example:

Game Boards:

1.

2.

3.

4.

5.

6.

Mike, Anita, and Jamal

162

Mike, Anita, and Jamal ate dessert. Read each clue. Then, mark the chart to see who ate which dessert.

Clues:

✔ Mike did not eat a candy bar.

✔ Jamal did not eat ice cream or a candy bar.

Example:

	Walk	Run	Jump
Mary		X	X
Seth	X	X	
Rich	X		X

Chart:

	Candy Bar	Ice Cream	Cake
Mike			
Anita			
Jamal			

Answers:

What did Mike eat? _____

What did Anita eat? _____

What did Jamal eat? _____

What's Next?

163

Draw the shape that should come next.

○△○○△○○○△○○○○△○○○○ ___

How Old?

164

Brian is six years older than his younger brother.

The sum of their ages is the same as three times the younger brother's age.

How old are Brian and his brother? _____

_____

Super Stumper: Letter Box

165

Put the letters A, B, C, and D in the boxes so that:

- A is directly below D.
- C is directly above B.
- A is directly left of B.

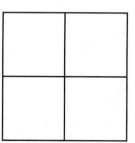

Letter Box

166

Put the letters A, B, and C in the boxes so that:

- A is directly left of D.
- A is directly above B.

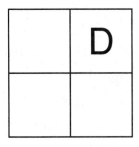

Eli's Shoes

167

Eli somehow lost his shoes! Can you help him find them? Circle the correct shoes. Here are facts about Eli's shoes:

 They are not high tops.

 They have laces.

 They have stripes.

Reversi

Directions:

1. Find a partner and two pencils.
2. One of you is **X**s and the other is **O**s.
3. Take turns marking your letter (**X** or **O**) on the game board.
4. Try to trap your partner's letter between two of yours. If you trap a letter, it turns into yours—erase the trapped letter and replace it with your own.
5. At the end, the person with the most letters on the board wins!

Example:

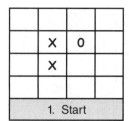
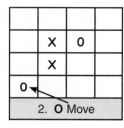
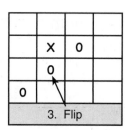
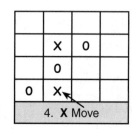
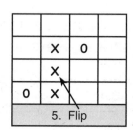

Game Board:

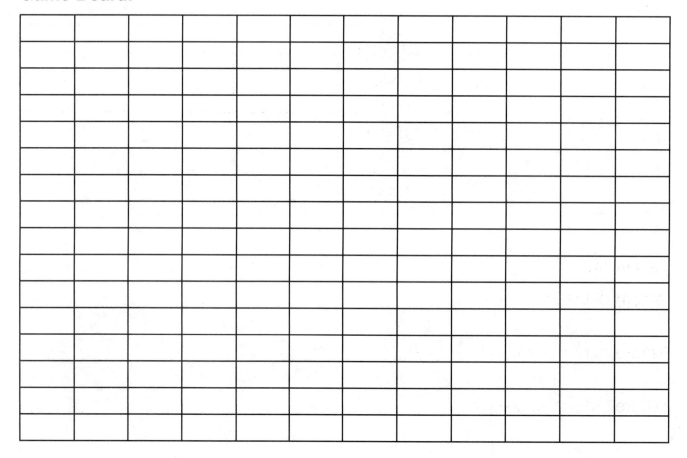

Mike, Anita, and Jamal

169

Mike, Anita, and Jamal went camping. Read each clue. Then, mark the chart to see where each person slept.

Clues:

✔ Mike slept in a bunkhouse.

✔ Anita did not sleep in an RV.

Example:

	Walk	Run	Jump
Mary		X	X
Seth	X	X	
Rich	X		X

Chart:

	Tent	Bunkhouse	RV
Mike			
Anita			
Jamal			

Answers:

Where did Mike sleep? _____

Where did Anita sleep? _____

Where did Jamal sleep? _____

170 What's Next?

Draw the shape that should come next.

△ ☐ ○ △ △ ☐ ○ △ △ △ ☐ ○ △ △ △ _____

171 How Old?

Kevin's sister is fifteen.

In four years, Kevin will be one year younger than his sister is now.

How old is Kevin? _____

172 Odd Animal Out

Circle the animal that does not belong.

Why doesn't it belong? _____

Anna's Kite

173

Anna went to the park to fly her kite, but the wind blew it away. Can you help her find it? Circle the correct kite.

Here are facts about Anna's kite:

✔ It is striped.

✔ It has three bows.

✔ It does not have flowers on it.

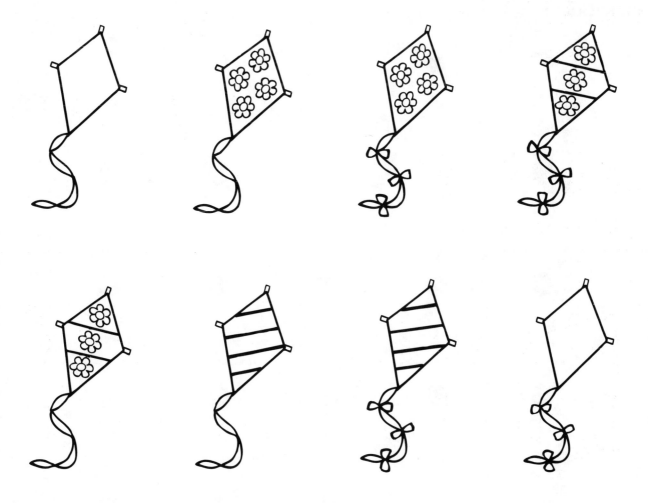

Blocked

174

Directions:

1. Find a partner and two pencils.

2. Take turns drawing lines from one dot to another. You can draw only vertical lines, and your partner can draw only horizontal lines.

3. Once any line touches a dot, the dot is closed and cannot be used again.

4. The first person who cannot make a move loses.

Example:

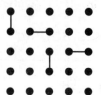

Game Board:

●　　●　　●　　●　　●

●　　●　　●　　●　　●

●　　●　　●　　●　　●

●　　●　　●　　●　　●

●　　●　　●　　●　　●

Mike, Anita, Jamal, and Kate

Mike, Anita, Jamal, and Kate ran a race. Read each clue. Then, mark the chart to see how each person finished the race.

Clues:

✔ Anita finished second.

✔ Kate finished ahead of Jamal, but behind Mike.

	1st	2nd	3rd	4th
Mike				
Anita				
Jamal				
Kate				

Answers:

How did Mike finish the race? _____

How did Anita finish the race? _____

How did Jamal finish the race? _____

How did Kate finish the race? _____

176 What's Next?

Draw the shape that should come next.

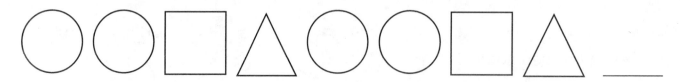

177 Letter Box

Put the letters A, B, and D in the boxes so that:

- A and D are in the same column.
- A and B are in the same row.

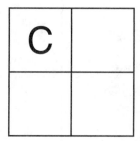

178 How Old?

Adam is four years older than his little brother.

In two years, Adam will be twice as old as his brother is now.

How old are Adam and his brother now? _____

_____

Hugo's Pizza

179

Hugo loves to eat pizza, but he does not like to order it. He always forgets to order all of his favorite toppings. Can you help him? Circle the correct pizza.

Here are facts about Hugo's pizza:

✔ Hugo always asks for pepperoni.

✔ Hugo always asks for mushrooms.

✔ Hugo never orders onions.

  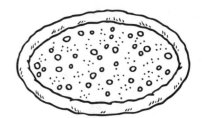

 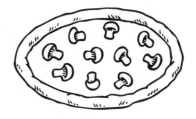

Boxed Out

Directions:

1. Find a partner. Each player should use a different-colored pen.

2. Look at the dots below.

3. Take turns drawing a short line between two dots.

4. Try to make closed boxes. When you make a box, color it in. Then, go again.

5. The person who makes the most boxes wins.

Example:

Game Board:

Mike, Anita, Jamal, and Kate

181

Mike, Anita, Jamal, and Kate have different favorite foods. Read each clue. Then, mark the chart to see who prefers which food.

Clues:

✔ Jamal and Anita like neither corn nor pizza.

✔ Jamal does not like cereal.

✔ Mike does not like corn.

	Corn	Cereal	Pizza	Apples
Mike				
Anita				
Jamal				
Kate				

Answers:

What is Mike's favorite food? _____

What is Anita's favorite food? _____

What is Jamal's favorite food? _____

What is Kate's favorite food? _____

What's Next?
182

Draw the shape that should come next.

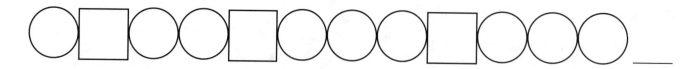

Letter Box
183

Put the letters A, B, and D in the boxes so that:

- C is directly below D.
- A and D are in the same row.

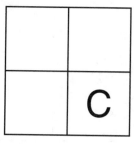

Odd Animal Out
184

Circle the animal that does not belong.

Why doesn't it belong? _____

185 What's Next?

Draw the shape that should come next.

186 Letter Box

Put the letters A, C, and D in the boxes so that:

- B and D are in the same column.
- A is in the bottom row.

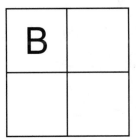

187 How Old?

In three years, Matt will be twice as old as his brother is now.

In three years, his brother will be eight.

How old are Matt and his brother now? _____

_____

Answer Key

Note: Answers are organized according to puzzle number, not page number.

Picture Puzzles

1.

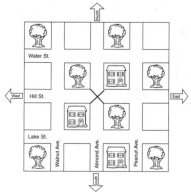

2.

3.

4. ten

6.

7. bigfoot

8. The horse with a hippo head is not a real animal.

9.

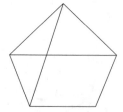

10. four things that do not belong: outboard motor, airplane, cell phone, and astronaut

12.

13. In the second picture, the winning dog has a spot, is not wearing a collar, and has an extra freckle. The second place dog is missing part of its tail. Also, the third place podium is a different height.

14.

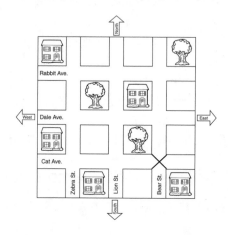

15.

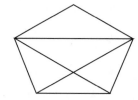

16. eggs over easy

17. The bee with a donkey's tail is not a real animal.

19.

20. two

21. The hawk with a dragon's tail is not a real animal.

22.

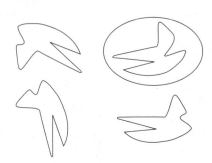

Answer Key *(cont.)*

23. In the second picture, the squirrel is missing, and five pinecones are hanging off of the tree. The fox is on the opposite side of the tree and is flipped around. The raccoon is also on the opposite side of the tree and is flipped around. In addition, the fox has no tail.

24. downtown

25.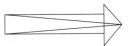

26. nineteen

27.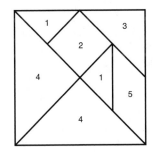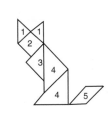
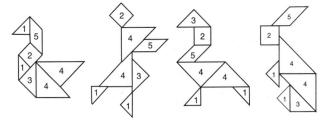

28.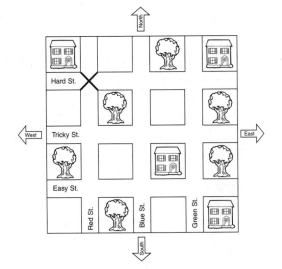

29. One little pig is wearing a hat, another has zebra stripes, and another is wearing sunglasses. In addition, the big pig has a bushy horse's tail.

30. thirty

31.

32. twelve

33. The fish with hands is not a real animal.

35. In the second picture, there is a dog in the background, the boy's hair is dark, the boy is wearing glasses and sandals (instead of being barefoot), and there is a different kind of sprinkler.

36.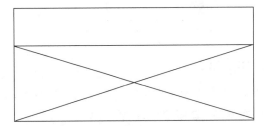

37. man overboard

38.

39.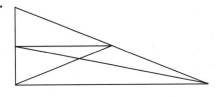

Answer Key (cont.)

41.

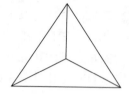

42. In the second picture, the cow is wearing a bell and has no horns. The cow also has spots, and its tail has moved. Finally, the moon has been repositioned.

43. eight

44.

45. The winged monkey is not a real animal.

46.

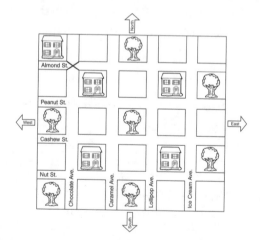

Word Puzzles

48. spit, tips, pits

49. a cheetah

50. DUCK

51. Charlotte requested a crown to cover her hairdo goof.

52. pit, stop, act, toast or oats, test, other, together

53. an eggzam

55. nope or open, no or on, stun, nine, need, nose

56. fist, fits, sift

57.

1 g	2 o	3 t
4 e	r	a
5 m	e	n

58. Catherine ran to and fro, going home.

59. BIRD

60. Answers will vary but may be similar to:

h	e	n
p	e	n
p	e	t
p	o	t

Answer Key *(cont.)*

61. Answers will vary but may include: comb, coach, coast, couch, cost, colt, tomb, toast, touch, toss, grouch, gross, bomb, boast, boss, bolt, feast, fess, felt, beach, beast, best, Bess, begin, belt

62. (You can't eat erasers or giant) cookies.

63. won or own, will, wing, mow, owl, bowl

64.

¹o	²f	³f
⁴a	i	r
⁵t	r	y

65. cats, scat, cast, acts

66. tag, soccer, hockey, cards

67.

		A						T
		L						E
		A						N
W	A	S	H	I	N	G	T	O	N
		K						E
A	L	A	B	A	M	A		S
					A			S
			O	H	I	O		E
					N			E
					E			

Other words will vary.

68. a lion

69. Fido got terrible fleas.

70. Answers will vary but may be similar to:

o	n	e
o	**w**	**e**
o	**w**	l
o	i	l

71. PIGGY

72. rip, wrapper, string, bring, stringer or stinger, strange or stranger, range, anger or ranger

73.

¹n	²e	³t
⁴o	a	r
⁵d	r	y

74. Ohio, Texas, Maine, Alaska

75. a quarter

76. Order may vary.

mouse → ear → rock → koala → apple → elf → fork → kangaroo → orange → elephant → train → nine

77.

¹o	²a	³t
⁴a	g	o
⁵k	e	y

Answer Key *(cont.)*

78. The (crowded) room (was packed) with (ogres!)

79. Answers will vary but may be similar to:

c	o	w
b	**o**	**w**
b	**o**	**g**
b	i	g

80. rat or art, car, start, raft, after, round

81. nets, sent, nest, tens

82. DOG

83. The (commando) granny told the (doc) to push with a (crowbar.)

84. pear, plum, apple, grape

85. Answers will vary but may include: through, thread, throat, thrifty, enough, enemy, although, spread, sprain, spring, bough, bead, boat, nifty

86. (Do girls have (pigtails?)

87. Answers will vary but may be similar to:

p	e	n
p	**e**	**g**
l	**e**	**g**
l	o	g

88.

t	a	n
a	g	o
g	e	t

89. step, pets, pest

Sentences will vary.

90.

t	h	e
e	e	l
a	r	f

91. the outside

92. snack, lunch, brunch, dinner

93.

w	e	b
i	v	y
g	e	e

95. it quacks up

96. camel, lion, zebra, rhino

97. BAT

98. act, cat

Sentences will vary.

Answer Key *(cont.)*

99.

¹b	²e	³l	⁴t
⁵o	v	e	r
⁶r	i	s	e
⁷e	l	s	e

100. Answers will vary but may be similar to:

r	i	s	e
r	**o**	**s**	**e**
h	**o**	**s**	**e**
h	o	m	e

101. Canada, France, Mexico, Italy

Number Puzzles

103.

1	4	3	2
3	**2**	1	4
2	1	**4**	3
4	3	2	**1**

104.

3	**7**	5	**5**	20
9	6	**3**	6	24
7	4	2	7	20
6	9	**4**	3	22
25	26	14	21	

105.

```
    1   6   9
+      [6]  7
  ───────────
   [2]  3  [6]
```

106.

7	**5**	**3**	**1**

107.

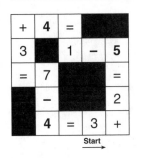

108. Answers will vary but may be similar to:

Player #1										Player #2								
1	2	③	4	5	6	7	8	⑨	**12**	9	⑧	7	6	5	④	3	2	1
1	2	3	④	5	6	7	⑧	⑨	**21**	9	8	⑦	⑥	5	4	3	2	1
1	②	3	4	5	6	7	⑧	⑨	**19**	9	8	⑦	⑥	⑤	4	3	2	①
1	2	③	4	5	6	⑦	⑧	⑨	**27**	9	⑧	⑦	⑥	5	④	3	②	1
1	2	3	④	5	⑥	⑦	8	⑨	**34**	9	⑧	⑦	⑥	⑤	④	③	2	1
1	2	3	4	5	6	⑦	8	⑨	**16**	9	8	⑦	⑥	5	4	3	②	1
1	②	3	4	5	6	⑦	⑧	⑨	**26**	9	⑧	⑦	6	⑤	④	3	②	1

109. 5

Paths will vary but may be similar to:

2	−	1
+	2	
2	+	

110.

5	**4**	3	1	**2**
4	33	5	21	3
3	5	**4**	2	**1**
1	21	2	24	5
2	**3**	1	**5**	4

111.

```
    1   6  [8]
+       8   7
  ───────────
  [2] [5]  5
```

112.

−	**9**	=	9	=
8		7		**5**
=		+		+
1		2↑ Start		4

113.

2	**4**	**5**	**8**

114.

2	**4**	1	**3**
1	3	**2**	4
3	**2**	4	**1**
4	1	3	2

Answer Key *(cont.)*

115. 2

Paths will vary but may be similar to:

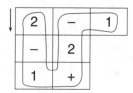

116.

5 + 13	2 x 7	8 − 5
18	14	3
72 − 34	34 + 17	4 x 9
38	51	36
56 + 32	84 − 43	2 x 3
88	41	6

31 + 47	4 x 6	22 − 16
78	24	6
3 − 2	33 − 22	7 x 8
1	11	56
7 x 4	18 + 26	31 − 14
28	44	17

53 − 35	32 + 23	3 x 9
18	55	27
6 x 4	16 + 26	91 − 19
24	42	72
1 x 21	82 − 28	22 + 34
21	54	56

42 + 49	33 − 16	4 x 8
91	17	32
28 − 17	8 x 5	52 + 23
11	40	75
5 x 7	14 + 18	66 − 33
35	32	33

117.

3	5	3		11
4	2	5		11
8	7	4		19

15	14	12

118.

3	2	5	1	4
1	23	2	23	3
2	5	3	4	1
4	27	4	24	5
5	3	1	4	2

119.

3	5	5	4

120.

3	5	7
+	9	9
4	5	**6**

121.

Start →

7	−	2	=
=	■	■	5
9	■	■	+
−	16	=	11

122.

1	3	2	**4**
2	**4**	1	3
4	1	**3**	2
3	2	4	1

123.

2	6	4		12
5	**6**	7		18
3	**5**	1		9

10	17	12

124. Answers will vary but may be similar to:

4	+	2	+	4	+	3
+	1	+	5	+	4	+
3	+	2	+	5	+	6
+	7	+	2	+	1	+
2	+	1	+	4	+	3
+	2	+	5	+	6	+
3	+	2	+	5	+	3

125.

3	7	9
+	4	3
4	2	**2**

126.

9	**6**	**5**	5

127.

Start ↓

7	+	**2**	=	9
=	■	■	■	−
5	+	2	=	7

128.

1	2	4	3
4	3	**1**	2
3	**1**	**2**	4
2	4	3	1

129.

1	**9**	**5**	15
6	3	**4**	13
2	**6**	5	13
9	18	14	

130.

2	3	**5**	4

131.

6	7	**7**

$$+ \quad 6 \quad 5$$

$$7 \quad \boxed{4} \quad 2$$

132.

+	2	=		
4		6↑ Start		3
=	**6**			=
	–			**2**
	1	=	5	–

133. Answers will vary but may be similar to:

	Player #1										Player #2									
2	③	4	5	6	7	8	⑨	⑩	**22**	10	9	⑧	⑦	6	⑤	4	3	②
②	3	4	5	⑥	7	⑧	⑨	⑩	**35**	⑩	9	⑧	⑦	6	⑤	4	③	②
②	3	4	⑤	⑥	⑦	⑧	⑨	⑩	**47**	⑩	⑨	⑧	⑦	⑥	5	④	③	2
②	3	4	5	6	7	⑧	⑨	⑩	**19**	10	9	8	⑦	⑥	5	④	3	②
②	③	4	5	6	⑦	⑧	⑨	⑩	**39**	⑩	⑨	⑧	⑦	6	⑤	④	③	②
2	3	④	⑤	⑥	⑦	⑧	⑨	⑩	**49**	⑩	⑨	⑧	⑦	6	⑤	④	3	②
②	③	4	5	6	7	⑧	⑨	⑩	**32**	⑩	⑨	⑧	7	6	⑤	4	3	2

134. 5

Paths will vary but may be similar to:

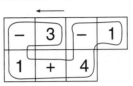

135.

3	2	**1**	4
1	4	3	2
4	3	2	1
2	**1**	4	**3**

136.

2	3	1	4	5
5	21	**3**	27	2
1	2	4	5	3
3	26	**5**	27	**4**
4	**5**	2	3	1

137.

2	**3**	4	9
2	6	**8**	16
7	7	**3**	17
11	16	15	

138.

8	+ or ⊖	3	⊕ or –	2	=	7
28	+ or ⊖	7	⊕ or –	9	=	30
32	+ or ⊖	12	+ or ⊖	5	=	15
19	⊕ or –	6	+ or ⊖	1	=	24
40	+ or ⊖	30	⊕ or –	10	=	20
16	+ or ⊖	1	+ or ⊖	8	=	7
25	⊕ or –	13	+ or ⊖	3	=	35
11	⊕ or –	4	⊕ or –	2	=	17

Answer Key *(cont.)*

139.

2	3	1	4
1	4	2	3
4	2	3	1
3	1	4	2

140. 2

Paths will vary but may be similar to:

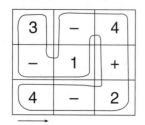

141.

5	9	2		16
6	2	4		12
4	2	6		12

15	13	12

142.

1	3	2	5	4
5	21	1	24	3
2	4	3	1	5
4	26	5	26	1
3	1	4	5	2

143.

2	8	4	6

144.

```
    5   5   7
 +      7   4
 ─────────────
    6   3   1
```

145.

8	=	2	+	6
−	■	7 Start ↓	■	=
1				3
=	■	+	■	−
7		2	=	9

146.

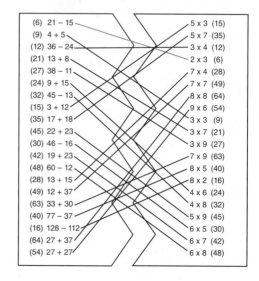

```
 (6) 21 − 15            5 x 3 (15)
 (9) 4 + 5              5 x 7 (35)
(12) 36 − 24            3 x 4 (12)
(21) 13 + 8             2 x 3 (6)
(27) 38 − 11            7 x 4 (28)
(24) 9 + 15             7 x 7 (49)
(32) 45 − 13            8 x 8 (64)
(15) 3 + 12             9 x 6 (54)
(35) 17 + 18            3 x 3 (9)
(45) 22 + 23            3 x 7 (21)
(30) 46 − 16           3 x 9 (27)
(42) 19 + 23           7 x 9 (63)
(48) 60 − 12           8 x 5 (40)
(28) 13 + 15           8 x 2 (16)
(49) 12 + 37           4 x 6 (24)
(63) 33 + 30           4 x 8 (32)
(40) 77 − 37           5 x 9 (45)
(16) 128 − 112         6 x 5 (30)
(64) 27 + 37           6 x 7 (42)
(54) 27 + 27           6 x 8 (48)
```

147.

3	1	8		12
4	2	9		15
8	4	7		19

15	7	24

148. 20

Paths will vary but may be similar to:

2	+	6
−	4	+
5	+	7

149.

2	3	4	1
4	1	2	3
1	2	3	4
3	4	1	2

Answer Key *(cont.)*

150.

4	**3**	7	2	16
6	5	2	**1**	14
2	**9**	3	5	19
8	4	**2**	6	20

20	21	14	14

Logic Puzzles

151. thirteen

152.

D	C
A	B

153. The spider does not belong because it has eight legs.

154.

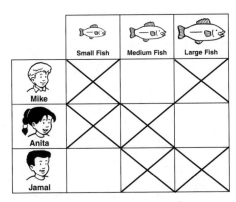

What fish did Mike catch? __the medium fish__

What fish did Anita catch? __the large fish__

What fish did Jamal catch? __the small fish__

156.

D	B
C	A

157. Jane has an analog watch with a striped band and a circular face.

158.

159. six

160. The sheep does not belong because it doesn't start with a "g." Or, the gorilla does not belong because it doesn't have hooves.

162.

What did Mike eat? __ice cream__

What did Anita eat? __candy bar__

What did Jamal eat? __cake__

163.

◯

164. Brian is twelve and his brother is six.

165.

D	C
A	B

166.

A	D
B	C

167. Eli has low-top shoes with laces and stripes.

Answer Key (cont.)

169.

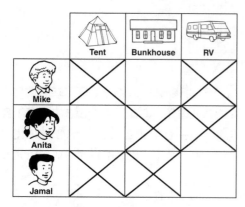

Where did Mike sleep? __the bunkhouse__

Where did Anita sleep? __the tent__

Where did Jamal sleep? __the RV__

170.

171. ten

172. The dolphin does not belong because it lives in the ocean, and it doesn't have fur.

173. Anna's kite has stripes and three bows.

175.

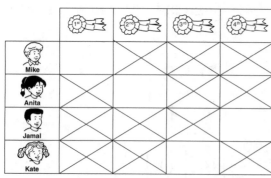

How did Mike finish the race? __in 1st place__

How did Anita finish the race? __in 2nd place__

How did Jamal finish the race? __in 4th place__

How did Kate finish the race? __in 3rd place__

176.

177.

C	D
B	A

178. Adam is ten and his little brother is six.

179. Hugo's pizza has pepperoni and mushrooms on it.

181.

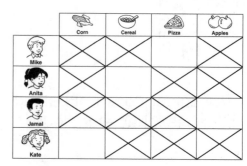

What is Mike's favorite food? __pizza__

What is Anita's favorite food? __cereal__

What is Jamal's favorite food? __apples__

What is Kate's favorite food? __corn__

182.

183.

A	D
B	C

184. The goat does not belong because it doesn't start with a "d." Or, the dinosaur doesn't belong because it is extinct.

185.

186.

B	C
D	A

187. Matt is seven and his brother is five.